DR. ANDERSON'S WORK ON THE HAWAIIAN ISLANDS.

BY ANDREW P. PEABODY, D.D., CAMBRIDGE, MASS.

[From the Boston Review for May, 1865.]

The Hawaiian Islands: Their Progress and Condition under Missionary Labors. By RUFUS ANDERSON, D.D., Foreign Secretary of the American Board of Commissioners for Foreign Missions. With Illustrations. Boston: Gould & Lincoln. 1864.

WE may profess implicit faith in the geological theories which adequately account for the condition and contents of the earth's crust; yet our faith in them lacks vividness, simply because no one of the world-forming processes has taken place under our own observation, or under the eye of witnesses who have told us their story. But were there at this moment an unfinished continent or island, still the abode of Saurian reptiles, or the laboratory of fossil coal, the fresh record of explorations in that region would convert our cosmogony from a vague or dead belief into a clearly conceived and intensely realized system of nature.

There has been in the remote past a social, there has been a religious cosmogony, and the greatest difficulty in the way of correct apprehensions as to the origin of civilization, and as to the methods of growth in the primitive church, lies in our lack of realizing and satisfying conceptions of the elements involved in each separate problem. The history of civilization is wrapped in obscurity. The veil of the Dark Ages fell upon certain savage tribes that had the mastery of Europe; it rose upon those tribes, still, indeed, rude in many of the arts of life, but already in an advanced condition of culture and of potential refinement. When we go back to the earlier civilization, we are equally unable to ascend to its cradle and to define the first stages of its growth. Yet birth and source it must have had, heavenly or earthly, and we all have our theories of its genesis;

but we hold them loosely and impassively, because it is so utterly impossible for us to conceive of the transmutation of savage into civilized man. Thus also, there was a creative era of the Christian church, a period when the transition was made, often simultaneously by large numbers of men and women, from Paganism or from Jewish ritualism to a vital faith in the Gospel. Of this era we have numerous memorials in the New Testament. The Epistles are full of the controversies, cases of conscience, weaknesses, scandals, causes of apostasy, incident to this infantile condition. But, though we doubt not the inspiration of the sacred writers, we are apt to enter with but feeble appreciation into the details of their casuistry; many of the topics which they treat seriously seem to us too trivial for grave animadversion; and in not a few cases they recognize as perfectly consistent with a position in the church states of character and modes of conduct which we should regard as incompatible with the Christian name. We thus find it hard to conceive of the earlier portions of Christian history, and while we devoutly acknowledge in them the divine working, we fail to discern the phases of humanity which the record simply describes without interpreting them. But if, after an interval of many centuries, these primitive civilizing and Christianizing processes have been renewed in our own time, even on a comparatively small scale; if even in the least of the nations an organic revolution such as had passed out of human expectation is now nearly consummated, the spectacle has a profound interest equally for the student of history and for the expositor of the Sacred Word.

Such a spectacle is exhibited in the book before us. On merely philosophical grounds it is of unique value. It shows us the means and steps of civilization, the circumstances which favor or check its growth, the action upon it of ideas and institutions respectively, its relations of cause and effect to religious culture. It throws essential light on even the most recondite questions, such as that of the possibility of a nation's becoming civilized except by aid or influence from without, that of man's primitive condition upon the earth, that of his decline or progress from his first estate.

Equally instructive, as we hope to show in the sequel, will this book be found by the biblical scholar. Since reading it, we have understood the Epistles to the Corinthians better than ever before, and have been led, as by no merely critical study, to admire the prudence, sagacity, insight and foresight of the inspired author, no less than his tender forbearance and charity for the newly converted under their liability to the trail and soil of the worship they had abjured. At the same time, we have here full verification of the aggressive power of Christianity in circumstances in no wise favorable for its reception. We learn that it was not as the outgrowth of its own age that the Gospel found reception when first promulgated, but that it is the everlasting Gospel, endowed with like life-giving energy for all times and nations. We especially prize this testimony at a period when naturalism is attempting to sap the foundations of our faith. Other religions have shown themselves the congenial products of their own birthtime by the failure of all attempts to extend their empire, otherwise than by force, in subsequent generations. They grow for a while, rapidly it may be, because they embody and sanction ideas level with the culture of their age; but as the race advances, or changes without advancing, they have no hold, except on the populations which they have educated, and cramped and dwarfed in educating them. A divinely given religion alone can be free from these limitations of time and race, and can work in the eternal freshness of its power on minds of every grade and of every form of culture.

But, most of all, as lovers of mankind, do we rejoice in the evidence here given of a new Pentecost of Christian salvation, in the assurance of the birth into the eternal life of thousands of perishing souls, in the establishment of the reign of Christ upon the ruins of savage fetichism, in the songs of Zion that have replaced the cannibal's war-whoop, in the altars of redemption railed with the broken spears of fierce idolators, in the homes that from beastly dens have become nurseries for heaven.

We should incur the charge of extravagance were we to attempt to convey the impression made upon us by Dr. Anderson's book. His tour among the Hawaiian Islands seems to us the most magnificent progress recorded in history; and his simple, modest narrative, so entirely devoid of egotism and of exaggeration, only makes us feel the more profoundly the greatness of his mission and the preëminent fitness of the agent. Dr.

Anderson in his youth devoted himself in purpose to the career of a foreign missionary, and from the time when he first found the Gospel precious to his own soul, the needs and claims of the unevangelized have never been absent from his thought. In the pendency of arrangements for an Eastern mission, he accepted a temporary clerical appointment on the staff of the American Board. This appointment was soon made permanent; after eight years of service as Assistant Secretary, on the death of Rev. Dr. Cornelius, in 1832, he became one of the three Corresponding Secretaries; and for nearly thirty years he has held the first place in the administration of that noble charity. It is not easy to tell what fertility of resource, what sagacity in the discernment of character, what world-wide knowledge, what executive ability, what hold upon the confidence of good men in all lands, what extended power of influence, have been needed and developed in a life like his. On his prudence, patience, judgment, energy, the entire system has depended, to a degree most fully appreciated by those who have been most intimately conversant with his labors. No statesman or diplomatist has held in his hands so many threads of affairs, often delicate and complicated, often of decisive moment, often involving even grave national interests, demanding with the directness and integrity that befit the servant of the Most High a fully equal measure of the subtile skill and adroit management, in which the children of this world are so apt to surpass the children of the light, and for lack of which a large portion of the philanthropy which has the purest record in heaven leaves no enduring traces of itself on earth.

When Dr. Anderson entered on his official duties, the second instalment of missionaries to the Hawaiian Islands had been despatched, many of the natives were under hopeful training, the language had been reduced to its alphabetic elements, and the first essays at printing had been successfully made. But at that time the mission was a still doubtful experiment. Shortly afterward, the regent and nine of the principal chiefs were gathered into the Christian church, vast multitudes were awakened to a lively interest in the Gospel, and the transformation of institutions, habits, domestic and social life took place so rapidly as to leave no longer room for fear of the reëstablishment of idolatry. During Dr. Anderson's secretaryship more than a hundred missionaries, clerical and lay, male and female, have been sent to the Islands from the United States, under his instruction and direction; while to the Home Board have been constantly referred vital questions of policy and administration, both civil and ecclesiastical, involving difficult relations with the emissaries and officers of foreign governments, and with missionaries, sometimes intrusive, from other religious bodies. Less than the soundest discretion, the most determined vigor, and the most watchful and persistent assiduity on the part of the American Board would at various crises of the mission have placed its interests at fearful hazard, and occasioned disastrous decline in the religious condition of the natives.

In 1862, the Hawaiian people was deemed to hold its rightful place among Christian nations, and the question was raised as to the gradual withdrawal of the support of the Board, with the view of leaving the Islands to support their own religious institutions, and to furnish their own Christian teachers. To ascertain data for the safe and judicious settlement of this question it was thought desirable to send an officer of the Board to the Islands, and especially fitting was it to delegate this commission to him who had for nearly forty years identified himself with the work, and who could claim as his "children in the Lord" those thousands of redeemed and converted savages. It was for him an antepast of the blessedness of heaven. Seldom can he who sows in tears count on earth his ranks of ripened sheaves. Even in the ordinary Christian ministry, while the faithful servant of Christ is never without ground for encouragement and gratitude, a collective view of vast results is not often vouchsafed to him; and many there are who have effected so little to the outward eye compared with their longing and endeavor, that they go to their rest feeling that much of their strength has been spent for naught, and only in the day when the secrets of all hearts shall be revealed, will they know their share in the harvest-work. But as Dr. Anderson passed from village to village and from island to island, he was permitted to see in great part the accumulated fruits of his life-toil, multiplied tokens of a regeneration in which his had been the controlling mind, evidences of a work of grace in which he had been the favored instrument, whose magnitude is to be estimated not by past and present converts, but by the unborn multitudes that shall enter on their Christian heritage. He was everywhere received with the love and reverence due to a father in Christ; thanks to God for his visit were sung in that language so strange to his ear; his advent was rapturously welcomed by immense congregations of the natives; he united in the celebration of the Saviour's death, with larger bodies of believers than he can often meet in his own land; his words of faith and love, interpreted by his missionary brethren, were listened to with intense earnestness, and met with the most fervent response; and liberal contributions for the distribution of the Scriptures and the furtherance of the Gospel were pressed upon him by those so recently brought from darkness into God's marvellous light. It was, indeed, a triumphal march through this newly conquered province of the Redeemer's empire—how unspeakably blessed to one who felt so profoundly that in all these offerings of affection, gratitude and veneration he was but receiving tribute for the King of kings!

Trusting that most of our readers have sought or will seek for themselves the instruction and edification proffered by the book before us, we shall enter into none of the details of Dr. Anderson's journeyings and personal experiences, but shall confine ourselves to a brief sketch of the former and present condition of the Hawaiian people, and a discussion of a few of the many subjects of interest treated or suggested by the author.

The Hawaiian Islands are ten in number. The native inhabitants bear in color, features and language strong affinities to the Malays, from whom they were probably derived. The population, at the arrival of the first missionaries, was estimated at one hundred and thirty five thousand, that of Hawaii, the principal island, at eighty thousand. The people were in the lowest condition of savage life. Their genial climate and spontaneously fertile soil had precluded the development of even the rude arts, of which in higher latitudes necessity would have been the teacher. Their dwellings were utterly devoid of comfort; their clothing insufficient for decency. The rights of property were hardly recognized. Extortion on the part of the chiefs, mutual theft and robbery among the people, seem to have been the common law. Polygamy was habitual among all who could obtain and support a plurality of wives, and licentiousness prevailed to the very verge of promiscuous concubinage. Infanticide was so prevalent as to have led to a marked decline of the population, two thirds of the children that were born having been buried barely to avoid the trouble of bringing them up. Murders and crimes of violence were perpetrated almost without restraint; and human sacrifices were offered for the recovery of the king when sick, and as victims at his obsequies. The natural conscience seems to have been obliterated, and there was no trace of a recognized distinction between right and wrong.

The prevalent idolatry was of the coarsest and most senseless type, consisting in the worship of hideous images, with no idea even of their being symbols of unseen powers. This idolatry was extirpated, by a unique combination of circumstances, about the time of the embarkation of the first American missionaries. It was a case in which Satan successfully cast out Satan, through the mysterious working of Him who makes even the wrath and guilt of man to praise him. Among the superstitions inseparable from the national religion was a stringent *tabu* system, extending not only to sacred days, places and persons, but to the domestic habits. Women were forbidden to eat in the presence of their husbands, and were debarred from many of the choicest articles of diet, whether fruit, flesh or fish. The violation of these interdicts was punishable by death, and it was supposed that the offender who escaped human vengeance would be destroyed by the gods. Foreigners had introduced ardent spirits, and to all the other sins of this degraded race was now superadded the habit of beastly drunkenness. The female chiefs, when intoxicated, found courage to indulge in prohibited food. Their rank secured them from punishment at the hand of man, and they were not slow in discovering that no vindictive bolt was launched at their heads by the divinity they had outraged. This *tabu* system seems to have been the fundamental doctrine, the *articulus stantis vel cadentis ecclesiæ* of their creed, and, this proved false, they found themselves atheists. The destruction of their idols, the burning of their temples ensued; and the missionaries discovered, for the first time in the world, an utterly godless people.

It can not be denied that this condition of things offered a vantage-ground for the labors of the earliest Christian teachers, yet less than might seem at first thought. Had the people been far enough advanced in spiritual development to feel the need of worship or to crave objects of reverence, the *rasa tabula* thus presented would have been easily written over with the holy names of the Christian faith. But these conditions precedent of religious belief seem to have been wanting. The tablet was not there. Yet undoubtedly it was easier, humanly speaking, to create it, than it would have been to make a palimpsest. The resistance presented by the *vis inertiæ* of a race utterly *dead* in trespasses and sins was less than might have been opposed by vital and vigorous misbelief. The seeds of faith lie in the depraved heart, and the dew of the divine grace which alone can make them fruitful is seldom wanting to fervent prayer and faithful endeavor. But, this one feature excepted, the condition of the Hawaiians in 1820 presented as unpromising a field for evangelic culture as lay anywhere beneath the sun, and, compared with the primitive age of the church, an immeasurably less hopeful field than any of the communities to which the apostles carried the word of life.

What are they now? In the arts of civilized life their progress has been at least equal to their conscious needs. While the chiefs and many of the inhabitants of the towns have well-built and well-furnished houses, the squalidness and misery of the rural districts and the poorer classes have given place to habits of decency and self-respect. The government has a written Constitution, with a Bill of Rights as liberal as that of Massachusetts, and with the powers of king, legislature and judiciary carefully defined and limited. The laws are wise, equitable, and preëminently Christian, guarding the religious liberty of the people, but providing against the desecration of the Sabbath and against the renewal of idolatrous superstitions and observances. The courts are admirably organized, and the judicial offices filled by men of competent ability and proved integrity, in part by native citizens, one of the three judges of the Supreme Court being a Hawaiian. There is no country in Christendom, in which life and property are more secure, and none in which the laws against intemperance and licentiousness are more vigilantly and rigidly executed. In the native language there have been published twenty thousand copies of the entire Bible, twelve thousand of the New Testament, and more than two hundred works beside, including school-books, books of religious instruction, and general literature. Three Hawaiian newspapers are issued. The Report of 1849 gives two hundred and eighty nine schools, with eight thousand six hundred and twenty eight scholars. There are several boarding schools, both for boys and girls, at which a superior education is afforded, and a High School, which would bear comparison with our best New England academies, and which has graduated nearly eight hundred pupils, ten of whom have been ordained as ministers of the Gospel. Algebra, Geometry, Trigonometry, Surveying and Political Economy are among the higher branches of learning which have been successfully taught. The people manifest a singular aptness for the acquisition of knowledge, and display an equal susceptibility for the ideas, impressions, tastes and habits which belong of right to advancing intellectual culture.

We can not need to say that this social renovation has been, not only coincident with and incidental to, but commensurate with and dependent upon, the action of Christian truth on individual hearts, and through them on the great heart of the nation. The history of that people for the last forty years has been a multiform commentary on the text: "The entrance of Thy word giveth light." As regards domestic and social habits, we have no evidence that the missionaries have busied themselves especially in the details of improvement. But the Christian consciousness is quick and keen in detecting incongruities and improprieties; the æsthetic nature is stimulated, nourished and instructed by the Divine Spirit, which is the Spirit of beauty no less than of grace; and the consecration of the body and all that pertains to the outward life, by purity, decency, neatness and order, can hardly fail to accompany or follow the consecration of the soul to the service of God. This exterior reformation must needs bear a close proportion, in its extent and thoroughness, to the energy of the work of grace. In these Islands the Gospel had from the first free course among the chiefs and the men and women of commanding influence, and its power was early felt through the whole people. In 1838 there was a great awakening throughout the entire nation, which resulted in the accession of many thousands of genuine converts to the churches. In 1843 more than a fourth part of the entire population were professing Christians; a larger proportion, it is believed, than could be found anywhere else in Christendom. To all these the missionary stations were centres of light, places of familiar resort, seminaries for instruction in things secular no less than in things spiritual. The superior fitness of the habits and appliances of civilized life was promptly perceived and felt; and the disciples, of necessity, became imitators of the teachers and their families in such portions of their mode of living as were applicable to their own condition. This last limitation is essential to a just estimate of the degree of their civilization. Had the missionaries themselves, with all their culture and refinement, belonged to a race for many generations domesticated in that climate, their artificial wants would have been much fewer and more simple; and it would seem to be the tendency of the great mass of their converts to adopt from them just such improvements as they need for decency and comfort, while those who from their position in the state are brought into more intimate relations with the foreign residents conform more fully to foreign tastes and habits. With this essential qualification the Hawaiians already merit a place among civilized nations—a much higher place than would be accorded to the Greeks with their glorious heritage and their little more than nominal Christianity; and they hold this position solely through the transforming power of religious faith and culture.

It is, also, because they have so readily received the divine word, that they have become to so extraordinary a degree an educated and a reading people. The Bible enlarges the mental horizon, suggests themes of thought, subjects of inquiry, gives a sacredness and a zest to knowledge of every kind, stimulates study, and generates mental activity. There evidently exists in this so lately benighted community a higher type of intellectual life, a more genuine love of learning, a surer promise of advanced and extended culture, than can be found in the mass of any people in Europe or America which is debarred free access to the oracles of divine truth.

As for the actual religious condition of these Islands, we have spoken of the proportion of church members in 1843. It is nearly or quite as large at the present time. In the judgment of Dr. Anderson and other equally intelligent witnesses, the evidences of sincere piety are as general and as satisfactory as among professed believers in any portion of Christendom.

Family prayer is almost universal among the converts. The Sabbath is kept sacred to an unusual degree, and its worship is attended by numerous, in some places, by vast congregations. Social prayer meetings are established in connection with every church, and are maintained with constancy, and often with zeal. The average moral character of the church-members is in most respects high, even by the standard of our older civilization, and the sins which have led to frequent ecclesiastical censure and excommunication, though more patent to rebuke, are certainly no more inconsistent with the spirit of our religion than the worldliness, penuriousness and meanness which pass unchallenged among the guests at our communion tables. Indeed, what indicates, perhaps, more clearly than all things else, the prevalent sincerity of these islanders is their readiness to give largely from their scanty means for the support and propagation of the Gospel. Their contributions average more than twenty thousand dollars annually, and their time and labor are always at the disposal of their teachers for the service of religion. In fine, though they not unfrequently show their still infantile estate as Christians, they at the same time exhibit abundant proof that the religion of the Gospel has wrought in thousands of hearts its regenerating work, and has so far leavened the entire community that there is no ground for apprehending a general apostasy or permanent decline.

We have dwelt on the evidences of their civilization, mainly with reference to the question which it was Dr. Anderson's special purpose to investigate, namely, the expediency of treating them as an integral part of Christendom, and gradually withdrawing from them the special tutelage of the Missionary Board. Their higher or lower degree of civilization or culture may not affect their present condition as Christians; but in their capacity to transmit that condition it is a vital element. The soul of the rudest savage may be converted to God and prepared for heaven; but the light that is in him can shed very little radiance around him. Christian institutions alone can perpetuate the power of the Gospel; and they can be sustained and extended among a population of unsettled habits and undeveloped intellect, only through the agency of a superior race. At most of our flourishing missionary stations the withdrawal of the missionaries would be followed by the speedy extinction of all Christian life. A self-perpetuating church implies the establishment of permanent homes and regular modes of industry, a forethought adequate to provide for future exigencies, mutual confidence among fellow-worshippers, the capacity of combined and organized action, and the existence of means of education, and habits of mental industry sufficient to ensure a well-trained ministry and a supply of intelligent office-bearers and leaders in church affairs. A community of which all this could be affirmed is to all intents and purposes civilized, and has within itself resources for further advancement and higher attainment. And in this sense the Hawaiians are civilized. We care not whether they live in houses of grass or of stone, sleep on mats or beds, sit on the ground or on chairs, eat with their fingers or with forks. These matters have no concern with civilization, that is, with the culture which fits men to be citizens and fellow-citizens.

Christianity always tends to civilize a community; but in order to produce this result, it must establish its control over the ruling classes, must permeate the body politic, mould its institutions, preside over its legislation, govern its social intercourse, and, above all, give character to the relations between husband and wife, parent and child, master and servant. Where this work has been in a good measure accomplished, its consummation may be retarded by the prolongation of foreign influence, however beneficent. It is well neither for individual nor collective humanity to remain in tutelage when the period of maturity has been reached. Guardianship beyond its due term cripples and dwarfs the faculties of self-help which it has created. We must, therefore, acknowledge the wisdom of the action of the American Board, in relinquishing the immediate control of the religious interests of these Islands to their native and resident population. The Board still provides for the maintenance of the missionaries already established, most of whom have passed the prime of active usefulness. The counsel and influence of these tried, approved and trusted teachers will be of essential benefit in the transition from pupilage to self-government, while the churches, unburthened by the necessity of contributing to their support, will have no obstacle in the way of securing and compensating the services of native ministers. At the same time those recent heathen are encouraged themselves to enter on the field of missionary enterprise, and this most wisely; for among the means of grace giving is second only to prayer, as the American church has found in its own blessed experience. The superintendence of the Micronesian mission is to be entrusted to an executive board chosen by the Hawaiian Evangelical Association, the American Board continuing its pecuniary aid for such time and in such measure as may be found necessary.

We have thus far presented only the bright and hopeful aspects of the Christian cause on these Islands. Is there not a reverse side? That there is we could not doubt, even were our author silent with regard to it. But, with his perfect candor, Dr. Anderson suppresses nothing, and our readers will miss in his pages not one of the salient facts which have been employed with malign purpose and effect by the calumniators of the mission. We have not referred to these facts in discussing the self-sustaining capacity of the Hawaiian churches, because they are not of sufficient magnitude to have any important bearing on that question, any more than the short-comings, dissensions and corruptions of our New England Christianity have on its power to prolong its own existence, and, by aid from on high, to purify and elevate its own standard of faith and piety. But we will now look at the shades in the picture.

In the first place, it must be admitted that there remains among the Hawaiian Christians a certain proclivity to licentiousness and intemperance. We are grieved, but not surprised or shocked at this. It is what is to be expected in a people separated by hardly a generation from an utterly brutish state of manners and morals. Aside from the theological question of original sin, though casting essential light upon it, there can be no doubt as to the transmission of moral tendencies in families and races. Had one of Herod's children become a disciple of Christ, he would have been a disciple of a very different type from one of the family of Joseph of Arimathea. He might repeatedly, under stress of sudden and intense temptation, have shown his sonship according to the flesh to the vilest of men, yet without losing from his heart the evidence of his spiritual sonship. Just such is the case with a tribe or race of converts from the lower forms of paganism. There is a heritage of evil in their very constitution of body, mind and soul. Ages of slavery to the animal appetites have stimulated those appetites, and given them a natively larger influence over the active powers of the moral nature than they have in a people whose nature has been moulded by centuries of self-control and mental and religious culture. The Christian consciousness may be as genuine and as strong in the recent savage as in the descendant from an ancestry of saints; yet in the former case it will have to contend with a host of the powers of evil, which in the latter were resisted and overcome in the remote past, and have since fought only with blunted weapons and with crippled strength. It must be remembered, too, that the social sentiments and habits of decency and propriety, which are a most essential safeguard and help to the individual Christian, at least in the early stages of the religious life, are of gradual growth and of cumulative efficacy, and that they have but just begun to grow in the Hawaiian people. It is said by the Spirit of God to every subject of renewing grace, as it was said to Abraham, "Get thee out of thine own country, and from thy kindred, and thy father's house, unto a land that I will show thee"; and the reality, intensity and working power of his faith are to be tested, not by the distance yet to be measured to the promised land, but by his distance from his starting point. He who moves on his pilgrimage from an idolatrous country, from kindred steeped in swinish sensuality, from a father's house no better than a kennel, may find himself at the close of a long and faithful pilgrimage below the starting point of natural conscience and conventional morality, at which the child of a consecrated household hears and obeys the same call of God; yet in the eye of heaven he will have fought a good fight, and have finished a noble course, and his children may commence where he closed his career.

As we have intimated, the details in the volume before us at once receive light from, and reflect light upon, the apostolic epistles. In the churches at Corinth and in Asia, St. Paul certainly recognizes as brethren beloved, and praises for their proficiency and good gifts as Christians, persons who needed advice and warning as to the very rudiments of morality. At Corinth there had been gross violations of chastity among the disciples, and it would seem that even the Lord's Supper had been made an occasion of excess and drunkenness. In fine, there was in that church a condition of things incompatible, according to our modern notions, with the lowest concrete form of vital Christianity. Yet in his second epistle we discern manifest traces in these frail novices of a sensitiveness to rebuke, an accessibleness to the movements of contrite sorrow, indicating all that is implied in the apostle's words as to the depth of Christian feeling in their hearts and the reality of their conversion to God. "For behold this self-same thing, that ye sorrowed after a godly sort, what carefulness it wrought in you, yea, what clearing of yourselves, yea, what indignation, yea, what fear, yea, what vehement desire, yea, what zeal"! St. Paul, it must be borne in mind, in view of these moral infirmities of his converts, is slow to condemn, chary of excommunication, prompt and earnest in the restoration of offenders, aware all the while that, though "the iniquity of their heels" — the sins in which they were born and bred, yet which they have in purpose left behind them — may at times "compass them about," there may yet be on their hearts the unobliterated seal of the Spirit. We can not but agree with some of the missionaries, as cited by Dr. Anderson, that among these modern converts excommunication has been too frequent, especially as the excommunicated have in numerous instances passed from a church which would have tolerated, not their sin, but their bitterly repented sin, to the less discriminating mercies of Romanism, which, whatever may be its theories, practically makes the way of transgressors easy.

The same sensitiveness to rebuke, which St. Paul recognizes among the Corinthians, may be remarked among the Hawaiians. Says Dr. Anderson, "I was assured of cases where, after a terrible declension, the return had been with increased humility, experience, watchfulness, and zeal, so that the lapsed recovered ones became at length pillars in the church."

So far from looking upon lapses of this kind, though frequent, as a ground of discouragement, we rather regard them, viewed in all their aspects, as a hopeful omen. It is an immense gain that the community has reached a condition in which such cases of sin are exceptional and abnormal, are not numerous enough to constitute a characteristic feature of the Christian society or to defy its discipline, and are already the objects of unfeigned shame and contrition among the guilty, and of hearty reprobation among their associates. Moreover, this unfortunate liability, so far as it exists, seems to be confined chiefly to those who have been heathen and savages, and is not likely to be transmitted to their children except in a modified and controllable form and degree. The now rising generation, trained under the shadow of the domestic altar and the Christian sanctuary, educated by religious teachers, imbued from their tender years in the morality of the Gospel, and large numbers of them made in their youth hopeful subjects of Divine grace, will grow up under at least as favorable influences as those which surround the young persons in our own land whom we regard as the hope of the church. This future is already beginning to be realized. The pupils of the missionary schools are fast establishing a higher tone of character. Of the native ministers we are told that not one has shown himself unworthy of his sacred trust. The manifest tendency is toward an elevated standard of practical ethics.

In this connection we can not but attach great importance to the laws of the kingdom, not only or chiefly in their prohibitory or punitive function, but as declarative of the collective moral sense, and as educating the general conscience. From all that we can learn, we infer that in the legislation, and at the hands of the judiciary of the Islands, purity and temperance are as carefully guarded as they can be by human authority, and that those who violate them can be protected only by the secrecy of their guilt. The laws against the manufacture of intoxicating drinks and against their sale to native residents are peculiarly stringent and severe, and a very recent attempt to relax the penalty for their sale has been defeated by the vote of nearly three fourths of the legislature — a vote which, as passed after able and thorough discussion, we feel warranted in regarding as an authentic exponent of public opinion.

Does it not appear from these statements that the easily besetting sins of the Hawaiians are treated with greater severity and present better promise of their rapid decline, than the vices that infect the religious communities of older Christendom — the selfishness, avarice and virtual dishonesty, which are "the abomination of desolation" in the church of God, and hold in sordid slavery many who claim to be its very pillars?

A much more serious discouragement to missionary labor on this field might seem to be found in the decline of the native population. On this subject it is not easy to obtain trustworthy data, either as to the extent to which causes of depopulation have operated in former times, or as to the degree in which they are now arrested. Captain Cook estimated the population at four hundred thousand; but this was undoubtedly an over-estimate. The earliest official census, in 1832, gives one hundred and thirty thousand, three hundred and fifteen; the latest, in 1860, sixty nine thousand, eight hundred. But for the first four years of these twenty eight, the decrease was at the rate of more than four per cent. per annum, while for the last seven years it has been less than two thirds of one per cent. per annum. The vices introduced by foreigners held a prominent place among the causes of the rapid decline from the first discovery of the Islands till the arrival of the missionaries. The passion for strong drink made fearful ravages among the people; while the vile lusts of their visitors from civilized lands brought upon them even still more loathsome agencies of disease and death, and undoubtedly weakened the vital stamina of coming generations. There has been also at three different periods since the commencement of the century a visitation of devastating epidemics, though it would seem that the liability to diseases of this class is much less than in regions not lying under the salubrious influence of breezes from the sea. Infanticide and human sacrifices must also account in part for the diminished numbers of the people, and the former of these causes must have very gradually ceased with the progress of Christianity. Then too, though the rude and squalid habits of savage life are not incompatible with a moderate growth of population, improvements in dwellings, dress, and medical treatment can hardly fail to preserve many lives that would else have been sacrificed in infancy, by needless exposure, or by curable disease. On the whole, we can not but believe that future enumerations will present results of a much more favorable character than the past, and that through the blessing of Providence this mild, gentle, tractable and highly improvable people may maintain its name and place among the nations of the earth, as a monument of Christian philanthropy, as a luculent token of the fulfilment of the promises of God, and as a centre and source of light to populations on the islands and coasts of the Pacific still lying under the shadow of death.

But were the case otherwise, were the gradual extinction of

this people clearly foreseen, would there be any the less reason to rejoice in what has been accomplished, and to extend to the declining remnant of the nation all the offices of Christian love? The salvation of thousands upon thousands of souls will still have rewarded the toil and sacrifice of the church and its agents; the national decline will have been retarded by this ministry of mercy; and there will have been written a chapter of the world's religious history, which we believe will be transcribed in letters of light in the Lamb's book of life.

We refer to this last named contingency, not because we think it probable, but because it may present itself to some of our readers as inevitable. It is undoubtedly a beneficent law of the divine Providence that races of feeble vitality and capacity shall yield place by the operation of natural causes to races of superior physical and intellectual vigor; in fine, that the different regions of the earth shall gradually pass into hands that can subdue it, avail themselves of its resources and enjoy its uses. Under this law, no doubt, the aborigines of North America will ultimately disappear, and the humane policy which ought to have been pursued to them from the first would not have ensured their preservation in the land, though it would have averted the condemnation of blood-guiltiness from the European settlers. But the Hawaiians do not seem to fall necessarily under this law. Their constitution is adapted to their climate; their capacity to their soil. They are amply able to develop the resources of their territory, and to employ for the general benefit the advantages of their position. They thus far show themselves susceptible of cultivation, and have made more rapid progress than has elsewhere left its record in the history of the world. They may not, indeed, have within themselves the elements of a great people; but their cluster of islets can never become the seat of a great people. They could not, indeed, protect themselves by arms against any of the leading powers of Christendom; but we trust that they will guard their modest independence by the arts and virtues that belong to a Christian nation, and by pacific and beneficent relations of intercourse and commerce. Their insular and solitary position may save them from dangerous complications with more powerful states; they can not lie on the track of any future belligerents, or become the victims of wars other than their own; and the time has gone by for aggression or usurpation from abroad, without shadow of reason or pretence of right.

Another danger to which this people is exposed grows out of the influx of foreign residents. Much of the land is peculiarly adapted to the growth of the sugar-cane, while rice, coffee and cotton are successfully cultivated. These commodities are most profitably raised on large plantations, and the soil suited to their production is already furnishing a lucrative investment for the disposable capital of France, England and America; while the commerce of the Islands has of necessity been hitherto conducted to a very great degree by immigrants from the older commercial nations. To these dominant classes of foreigners there have been recently added importations of coolies from China for labor on the sugar-plantations. If enterprise on the one hand and manual labor on the other are to be permanently usurped by immigrants, of course under this double pressure the native population will inevitably decline in resources and in energy, and will be gradually absorbed and obliterated by intermarriage with the intrusive races. But whether this shall be the case or not must depend, we believe, on the thoroughness of the civilizing and Christianizing work which has been wrought upon the natives. If considerable numbers of them are fitted in intelligence and character to hold commanding positions, and to conduct extended operations in agriculture and commerce, they will in the lapse of one or two generations replace the foreign residents; for, with equal ability, they will have the advantage in physical constitution, in attachment to the soil, in the command of the language, and in the confidence of their fellow-countrymen. If, at the other extremity of the social scale, Christian culture develops habits of industry and creates a felt need of the comforts of civilized life, the mass of the people will not suffer the soil to be cultivated by strangers.

The labor of coolies, while on moral grounds little preferable to that of slaves, is not much less costly and wasteful, their nominally low wages being hardly an offset to the expense of importation and the rapid mortality among them; and the Hawaiians, once made aware of the duty and the privilege of toil, will readily demonstrate the superior economy of free labor. Much of the land planted with sugar-cane is now in the hands of small native proprietors; and on these estates free labor is proved to be amply remunerative. On the whole we can not believe that a people that deserves to live can be pressed down and crushed out on its own soil. Foreign enterprise has gained its ascendancy, and foreign labor its foothold in the Hawaiian Islands, only while the natives are in training to take effective possession of their birthright. If they show themselves mentally or morally unfit to retain the heritage, we doubt not that Providence will bestow it on races more worthy of it. But in what God has done for this people, while we may not presume to lift the veil from his decrees, we can not but trust that he has been training, not only souls for heaven, but a nation to serve him in the land which he has given to them.

Another topic, to which we are bound to allude, however unwillingly, in treating of the adverse or discouraging circumstances in connection with Hawaiian Christianity, is that of divided religious interests. In the older portions of Christendom, the phenomenon of rival sects is understood, and their common appeal to the same plenary and divine authority casts the weight of their combined testimony and influence on the side of faith. But those recently converted from heathenism, accustomed to uniformity of belief and worship in their previous estate, and knowing little of the history of the Christian church, are perplexed and often thrown into scepticism by the antagonisms of mutually exclusive sects. They can not comprehend the identity of religion where there is no community of religious interest and feeling. In their view the denial of the doctrines and the contempt of the ritual in which they have been trained are tantamount to the rejection and contempt of Christianity. Even in the age of the apostles, and under the ministry of those who had received their doctrine from the lips or by the revelation of the Lord, it was feared lest different modes of teaching and discipline on the same soil might be fraught with mischief. St. Paul expresses his determination not to enter on other men's labors, and laments and deprecates the consequences of the intrusion on his own ground of teachers not authorized or approved by himself. In the world-wide field open to the philanthropy of the church, modern Protestant missionaries have in general recognized this principle, and have been unwilling to present before heathendom the spectacle of a distracted church and a divided Gospel. When they could not labor side by side without collision or wide dissiliency of aim or action, they have, like Abraham and Lot, fed their flocks apart.

This Christian comity has been violated by the Mission of the English church, or, as it styles itself, the "Reformed Catholic Mission." The subject is one which we would gladly omit; but we should do injustice equally to the work under review and to the mission cause, were we to pass it over in silence.

The late king having become interested in the services of the English church, and there being at Honolulu many English residents who had been educated in its worship, application was made by Rev. Dr. Armstrong, once a missionary of the American Board, and then filling the office of President of the Board of Public Instruction, and Mr. Wyllie, an Englishman, Minister of Foreign Affairs, to Rev. William Ellis of London, pledging a moderate salary to some suitable English clergyman, who might consent to assume the pastorate of a church at the capital. The request was made for "a man with evangelical sentiment, of respectable talents, and most exemplary Christian life. A high churchman," added Dr. Armstrong, "or one of loose Christian habits, would not succeed. He would not have the sympathy and support of the other evangelical ministers at all, but rather opposition." This application was in entire accordance with the wishes of the missionaries and their friends, Indeed Dr. Anderson had previously urged a bishop of the American Episcopal church to sent out a presbyter of his diocese with reference to such a charge. Mr. Wyllie, who seems to have been playing a double game, had previously entered into correspondence with Mr. Hopkins, the Hawaiian consul in London, and a plan was matured through his agency for sending to the Islands a bishop and three presbyters, under the [high church] auspices of the Society for Propagating the Gospel. When this project became known, the American Board instituted a correspondence with the Archbishop of Canterbury and the Bishop of London, both of whom are understood to have sympathized with the views of the Board, and to have been opposed to intrusion on the field which they had made their own. But the counsels of the high church party prevailed. Bishop Staley was consecrated in 1861, and arrived at Honolulu, accompanied by two of his presbyters, and shortly followed by a third, in October, 1862.

These men of lofty apostolic pretensions have taken precisely the course which might have been anticipated, and will undoubtedly succeed in creating schism and animosity among the native Christians. They ignore the ministerial character and office of the American missionaries. They avail themselves of every opportunity of baptising children, without reference to the ecclesiastical relations of the parents. They have established the most showy and Romeward tending modes of worship, "with surplice and stole, with alb, and cope, and crosier; with rochet, and mitre, and pastoral staff; with Episcopal ring and banner; with pictures, altar-candles, robings, intonations, processions and attitudes." Meanwhile Bishop Staley has been preaching the most extreme and offensive doctrines of his party in the church, doctrines diametrically opposed to those taught by the missionaries, patristical tradition, baptismal regeneration, the gift of the Holy Spirit in confirmation, confession to the priest, and priestly absolution. At the same time he has stultified himself, while he has no doubt mystified his serious hearers, and encouraged the undevout in the desecration of holy time, by declaring that Sunday is "most falsely and mischievously called the Sabbath," and intimating that the daily service of the church and the observance of its solemn festivals fitly supersede the special reverence with which the people had been taught by the missionaries and required by the law of the land to regard the one day in seven. He has stultified himself, we say; for, unless the high church "has changed all this," the precept, "Remember that thou keep holy the Sabbath day," is read constantly in the ante-communion service, with the response, "Lord, have mercy upon us, and incline our hearts to keep this law." If Sunday is "most falsely and mischievously called the Sabbath," to what observance does this portion of the English liturgy have reference? Or does Bishop Staley require his adherents, in the most sacred service of the altar, to perform an act of solemn mockery, to offer a prayer which is arrant blasphemy, to beg of the divine mercy that they may be inclined to practice "falsehood and mischief"? Candles at noonday are a harmless folly; this is gross impiety.

The success of this mission has as yet been very limited. Its congregations are small. The modes of worship repel the simple tastes of such as have been sincerely attached to the ministrations of their earlier teachers; and those who want to be addressed through the senses, and gravitate toward the old idolatry, can find more that is congenial among the Roman Catholics than among their imitators. Yet under the patronage of the court and of some of the more influential foreign residents this superstition must needs grow. It can hardly fail to create a diversion from the interests of a simple faith and worship, which is especially to be deprecated at the present crisis, when the autonomy of the native church is just beginning, and needs the combined zeal, effort and liberality of all who love the cause of Christ and seek the prosperity of Zion.

We have spoken freely and warmly of this intrusion; but we believe that we have said no more than candid Episcopalians would readily admit and endorse. For the English church and its American sister we cherish all due reverence, gratitude and affection; and because we feel this, we can not think or write with easy tolerance of the stilted and popinjay caricatures of its solemn order and majestic ritual.

There is also on the Islands a Roman Catholic Mission, numbering as proselytes, (including all baptized persons,) more than twenty thousand souls. The Mormons have, too, a small settlement on the island of Lanai, and reckon, (including children,) not far from four thousand members. It does not appear that either of these forms of belief is making rapid progress, or presents any active hostility to the success of Protestant Christianity.

While we should be gratified to see this new-born people united in faith and worship, we can conceive that this diversity of ministration, these forms of error, these tares growing with the wheat, may be made subservient to their better proficiency in divine things. Inquiry, comparison, mental activity on religious subjects will be aroused and guided; the native pastors will feel the more intense need of taking heed to themselves, their doctrine and their flocks, because they are in the midst of gainsayers; private Christians will have added inducements to be loyal to the Master who can receive no wounds so deep as in the house of his friends; and thus a more intelligent faith and a more fervent piety may spring from the present division, and may prepare the way for the ultimate triumph of the truth over all obstacles and hindrances.

We have foreborne making extracts from the work under review, because we are unwilling that any of our readers should become acquainted with it in scraps or fragments. We have not even given an analysis of it, though our materials have been chiefly derived from it. Besides, there are no *especially* interesting extracts. The whole, from the Preface to the Appendix, is full of intense interest for all who love their Saviour and their race. The narrative flags not for one moment on the eager attention of the reader, nor can it fail to lift the devout heart as with a continuous anthem of praise to Him who has "given such power unto men," as is shown forth in this regenerated people.

One thought suggests itself in conclusion. Much of the science of our day busies itself, with a depraved ingenuity, in detaching man's hold on the ancestral tree by which he traces his descent from God, and of which, among the progeny of the second Adam, he may become a living branch. The true answer to these speculations is not to be found in ethnology or in physiology. No race can make out an unbroken pedigree; nor yet can we deny that there are strong analogies between the higher orders of quadrupeds and the lower members of the human family, not only in physical structure, but in mental capacity. Fifty years ago, the half-reasoning elephant or the tractable and troth-keeping dog might have seemed the peer, or more, of the unreasoning and conscienceless Hawaiian. From that very race, from that very generation, with which the nobler brutes might have scorned to claim kindred, have been developed the peers of saints and angels. Does not the susceptibility of regeneration, the capacity for all that is tender, beautiful and glorious in the humanity of the Lord from heaven — inherent in the lowest types of our race — of itself constitute an impassable line of demarcation between the brute and man? Has physical science a right to leave "the new man in Christ Jesus," which the most squalid savage may become, out of the question in its theories of natural selection or spontaneous development? When the modern Lucretianism can account for the phenomena of Christian salvation, without the intervention of miracle, revelation, or Redeemer, and not till then, can it demand our respect as a tenable theory of the universe.

www.ingramcontent.com/pod-product-compliance
Lightning Source LLC
LaVergne TN
LVHW011145110826
845150LV00008B/2517

9781418192181